Ion by Euripides

Translated from the Greek by Robert Potter

Euripides is rightly lauded as one of the great dramatists of all ti... ...e, he wrote over 90 plays and although only 18 have survived they reveal the scope and reach of his genius.

Euripides is identified with many theatrical innovations that have influenced drama all the way down to modern times, especially in the representation of traditional, mythical heroes as ordinary people in extraordinary circumstances.

As would be expected from a life lived 2,500 years ago, details of it are few and far between. Accounts of his life, written down the ages, do exist but whether much is reliable or surmised is open to debate.

Most accounts agree that he was born on Salamis Island around 480 BC, to mother Cleito and father Mnesarchus, a retailer who lived in a village near Athens. Upon the receipt of an oracle saying that his son was fated to win "crowns of victory", Mnesarchus insisted that the boy should train for a career in athletics.

However, what is clear is that athletics was not to be the way to win crowns of victory. Euripides had been lucky enough to have been born in the era as the other two masters of Greek Tragedy; Sophocles and Æschylus. It was in their footsteps that he was destined to follow.

His first play was performed some thirteen years after the first of Socrates plays and a mere three years after Æschylus had written his classic The Oristria.

Theatre was becoming a very important part of the Greek culture. The Dionysia, held annually, was the most important festival of theatre and second only to the fore-runner of the Olympic games, the Panathenia, held every four years, in appeal.

Euripides first competed in the City Dionysia, in 455 BC, one year after the death of Æschylus, and, incredibly, it was not until 441 BC that he won first prize. His final competition in Athens was in 408 BC. The Bacchae and Iphigenia in Aulis were performed after his death in 405 BC and first prize was awarded posthumously. Altogether his plays won first prize only five times.

Euripides was also a great lyric poet. In Medea, for example, he composed for his city, Athens, "the noblest of her songs of praise". His lyric skills however are not just confined to individual poems: "A play of Euripides is a musical whole....one song echoes motifs from the preceding song, while introducing new ones."

Much of his life and his whole career coincided with the struggle between Athens and Sparta for hegemony in Greece but he didn't live to see the final defeat of his city.

Euripides fell out of favour with his fellow Athenian citizens and retired to the court of Archelaus, king of Macedon, who treated him with consideration and affection.

At his death, in around 406BC, he was mourned by the king, who, refusing the request of the Athenians that his remains be carried back to the Greek city, buried him with much splendor within his own dominions. His tomb was placed at the confluence of two streams, near Arethusa in Macedonia, and a cenotaph was built to his memory on the road from Athens towards the Piraeus.

Index of Contents

THE PERSONS

MERCURY
ION
CREUSA, daughter of Erechtheus
XUTHUS, husband of CREUSA
TUTOR
ATTENDANT
PRIESTESS OF APOLLO
MINERVA
CHORUS OF HANDMAIDENS OF CREUSA

SCENE

Before the Temple of Apollo at Delphi. The sun is about to rise.

ION

MERCURY enters.

MERCURY
Atlas, that on his brazen shoulders rolls
Yon heaven, the ancient mansion of the gods,
Was by a goddess sire to Maia; she
To supreme Jove bore me, and call'd me Hermes;
Attendant on the king, his high behests
I execute. To Delphi am I come,
This land where Phoebus from his central throne
Utters to mortals his high strain, declaring
The present and the future; this is the cause;
Greece hath a city of distinguish'd glory,
Which from the goddess of the golden lance

Received its name; Erechtheus was its king;
His daughter, call'd Creusa, to the embrace
Of nuptial love Apollo strain'd perforce,
Where northward points the rock beneath the heights
Crown'd with the Athenian citadel of Pallas,
Call'd Macrai by the lords of Attica.
Her growing burden, to her sire unknown
(Such was the pleasure of the god,) she bore,
Till in her secret chamber to a son
The rolling months gave birth: to the same cave,
Where by the enamour'd god she was compress'd,
Creusa bore the infant: there for death
Exposed him in a well-compacted ark
Of circular form, observant of the customs
Drawn from her great progenitors, and chief
From Erichthonius, who from the Attic earth
Deriv'd his origin: to him as guards
Minerva gave two dragons, and in charge
Consign'd him to the daughters of Aglauros:
This rite to the Erechthidae hence remains,
Mid serpents wreathed in ductile gold to nurse
Their children. What of ornament she had
She hung around her son, and left him thus
To perish. But to me his earnest prayer
Phoebus applied, "To the high-lineaged sons
Of glorious Athens go, my brother; well
Thou know'st the city of Pallas; from the cave
Deep in the hollow rock a new-born babe,
Laid as he is, and all his vestments with him;
Bring to thy brother to my shrine, and place
At the entrance of my temple; of the rest
(For, know, the child is mine) I will take care."
To gratify my brother thence I bore
The osier-woven ark, and placed the boy
Here at the temple's base, the wreathed lid
Uncovering, that the infant might be seen.
It chanced, as the orient sun the steep of heav'n
Ascended, to the god's oracular seat
The priestess entering, on the infant cast
Her eye, and marvelled, deeming that some nymph
Of Delphi at the fane had dared to lay
The secret burden of her womb: this thought
Prompts her to move it from the shrine: but soon
To pity she resign'd the harsh intent;
The impulse of the god secretly acting
In favour of the child, that in his temple
It might abide; her gentle hand then took it,
And gave it nurture; yet conceived she not

That Phoebus was the sire, nor who the mother
Knew aught, nor of his parents could the child
Give information. All his youthful years
Sportive he wandered round the shrine, and there
Was fed: but when his firmer age advanced
To manhood, o'er the treasures of the god
The Delphians placed him, to his faithful care
Consigning all; and in this royal dome
His hallow'd life he to this hour hath pass'd.
Meantime Creusa, mother of the child,
To Xuthus was espoused, the occasion this:-
On Athens from Euboean Chalcis roll'd
The waves of war; be join'd their martial toil,
And with his spear repell'd the foe; for this
To the proud honour of Creusa's bed
Advanc'd; no native, in Achaea sprung
From Aeolus, the son of Jove. Long time
Unbless'd with children, to the oracular shrine
Of Phoebus are they come, through fond desire
Of progeny: to this the god hath brought
The fortune of his son, nor, as was deem'd,
Forgets him; but to Xuthus, when he stands
This sacred seat consulting, will he give
That son, declared his offspring; that the child,
When to Creusa's house brought back, by her
May be agnized; the bridal rites of Phoebus
Kept secret, that the youth may claim the state
Due to his birth, through all the states of Greece
Named Ion, founder of the colonies
On the Asiatic coast. The laurell'd cave
Now will I visit, there to learn what fortune
Is to the boy appointed, for I see
This son of Phoebus issuing forth to adorn
The gates before the shrine with laurel boughs.
First of the gods I hail him by the name
Of Ion, which his fortune soon will give him.

[**MERCURY** vanishes. **ION** and the attendants of the temple enter.]

ION [chanting]
Now flames this radiant chariot of the sun
High o'er the earth, at whose ethereal fire
The stars into the sacred night retreat:
O'er the Parnassian cliffs the ascending wheels
To mortals roll the beams of day; the wreaths
Of incense-breathing myrrh mount to the roof
Of Phoebus' fane; the Delphic priestess now
Assumes her seat, and from the hallow'd tripod

Pronounces to the Greeks the oracular strains
Which the god dictates. Haste, ye Delphic train,
Haste to Castalia's silver-streaming fount;
Bathed in its chaste dews to the temple go;
There from your guarded mouths no sound be heard
But of good omen, that to those who crave
Admission to the oracle, your voice
May with auspicious words expound the answers.
My task, which from my early infancy
Hath been my charge, shall be with laurel boughs
And sacred wreaths to cleanse the vestibule
Of Phoebus, on the pavement moistening dews
To rain, and with my bow to chase the birds
Which would defile the hallow'd ornaments.
A mother's fondness, and a father's care
I never knew: the temple of the god
Claims then my service, for it nurtured me.

[The **ATTENDANTS** leave. **ION** busies himself before the temple as he continues to sing., strophe]

Haste, thou verdant new-sprung bough,
Haste, thy early office know;
Branch of beauteous laurel come,
Sweep Apollo's sacred dome,
Cropp'd this temple's base beneath,
Where the immortal gardens breathe,
And eternal dews that round
Water the delicious ground,
Bathe the myrtle's tresses fair.
Lightly thus, with constant care,
The pavement of the god I sweep,
When over the Parnassian steep
Flames the bright sun's mounting ray;
This my task each rising day.
Son of Latona, Paean, Paean, hail!
Never, O never may thy honours fail!

[antistrophe]

Grateful is my task, who wait
Serving, Phoebus, at thy gate;
Honouring thus thy hallow'd shrine,
Honour for the task is mine.
Labouring with unwilling hands,
Me no mortal man commands:
But, immortal gods, to you
All my pleasing toil is due.
Phoebus is to me a sire;

Grateful thoughts my soul inspire;
Nurtured by thy bounty here,
Thee, Apollo, I revere;
As a father's I repeat.
Son of Latona, Paean, Paean, hail!
Never, O never may thy honours fail!

Now from this labour with the laurel bough
I cease; and sprinkling from the golden vase
The chaste drops which Castalia's fountain rolls,
Bedew the pavement. Never may I quit
This office to the god; or, if I quit it,
Be it, good Fortune, at thy favouring call!
But see, the early birds have left their nests,
And this way from Parnassus wing their flight.
Come not, I charge you, near the battlements,
Nor near the golden dome. Herald of Jove,
Strong though thy beak beyond the feather'd kind,
My bow shall reach thee. Towards the altar, see,
A swan comes sailing: elsewhere wilt thou move
Thy scarlet-tinctured foot? or from my bow
The lyre of Phoebus to thy notes attuned
Will not protect thee; farther stretch thy wings;
Go, wanton, skim along the Delian lake,
Or wilt thou steep thy melody in blood.
Look, what strange bird comes onwards; wouldst thou fix
Beneath the battlements thy straw-built nest?
My singing bow shall drive thee hence; begone,
Or to the banks of Alpheus, gulfy stream,
Or to the Isthmian grove; there hatch thy young;
Mar not these pendent ornaments, nor soil
The temple of the god: I would not kill you:
'Twere pity, for to mortal man you bear
The message of the gods; yet my due task
Must be perform'd, and never will I cease
My service to the god who nurtured me.

[The **CHORUS** enters. The following lines between **ION** and the **CHORUS** are chanted responsively as they gaze admiringly at the decorations on the temple.]

CHORUS
The stately column, and the gorgeous dome
Raised to the gods, are not the boast alone
Of our magnificent Athens; nor the statues
That grace her streets; this temple of the god,
Son of Latona, beauteous to behold,
Beams the resplendent light of both her children.

ION
Turn thine eyes this way; look, the son of Jove
Lops with his golden scimitar the heads
Of the Lernean Hydra: view it well.

CHORUS
I see him.

ION
And this other standing nigh,
Who snatches from the fire the blazing brand.

CHORUS
What is his name? the subject, on the web
Design'd, these hands have wrought in ductile gold.

ION
The shield-supporting Iolaus, who bears
The toils in common with the son of Jove.
View now this hero; on his winged steed
The triple-bodied monster's dreadful force
He conquers through the flames his jaws emit.

CHORUS
I view it all attentively.

ION
Observe
The battle of the giants, on the walls
Sculptured in stone.

CHORUS
Let us note this, my friends.

ION
See where against Enceladus she shakes
Her gorgon shield.

CHORUS
I see my goddess, Pallas.

ION
Mark the tempestuous thunder's flaming bolt
Launch'd by the hand of Jove.

CHORUS
The furious Mimas
Here blazes in the volley'd fires: and there

Another earth-born monster falls beneath
The wand of Bacchus wreathed with ivy round,
No martial spear. But, as 'tis thine to tend
This temple, let me ask thee, is it lawful,
Leaving our sandals, its interior parts
To visit?

ION
Strangers, this is not permitted.

CHORUS
Yet may we make inquiries of thee?

ION
Speak;
What wouldst thou know?

CHORUS
Whether this temple's site
Be the earth's centre?

ION
Ay, with garlands hung,
And gorgons all around.

CHORUS
So fame reports.

ION
If at the gate the honey'd cake be offer'd,
Would you consult the oracle, advance
To the altar: till the hallow'd lamb has bled
In sacrifice, approach not the recess.

CHORUS
I am instructed: what the god appoints
As laws, we wish not to transgress: without
Enough of ornament delights our eyes.

ION
Take a full view of all; that is allow'd.

CHORUS
To view the inmost shrine was our lord's order.

ION
Who are you call'd? Attendants on what house?

CHORUS
Our lords inhabit the magnific domes
Of Pallas.-But she comes, of whom thou askest.

[**CREUSA** and attendants enter.]

ION
Lady, whoe'er thou art, that liberal air
Speaks an exalted mind: there is a grace,
A dignity in those of noble birth,
That marks their high rank. Yet I marvel much
That from thy closed lids the trickling tear
Water'd thy beauteous cheeks, soon as thine eye
Beheld this chaste oracular seat of Phoebus.
What brings this sorrow, lady? All besides,
Viewing the temple of the god, are struck
With joy; thy melting eye o'erflows with tears.

CREUSA
Not without reason, stranger, art thou seized
With wonder at my tears: this sacred dome
Awakes the sad remembrance of things past.
I had my mind at home, though present here.
How wretched is our sex! And, O ye gods,
What deeds are yours! Where may we hope for right,
If by the injustice of your power undone?

ION
Why, lady, this inexplicable grief?

CREUSA
It matters not; my mind resumes its firmless:
I say no more; cease thy concern for me.

ION
But say, who art thou? whence? what country boasts
Thy birth? and by what name may we address thee?

CREUSA
Creusa is my name, drawn from Erechtheus
My high-born lineage; Athens gave me birth.
Illustrious is thy state; thy ancestry
So noble that I look with reverence on thee.

CREUSA
Happy indeed is this, in nothing farther.

ION

But tell me, is it true what fame has blazon'd?

CREUSA
What wouldst thou ask? Stranger, I wish to know.

ION
Sprung the first author of thy line from the earth?

CREUSA
Ay, Erichthonius; but my race avails not.

ION
And did Minerva raise him from the earth?

CREUSA
Held in her virgin hands: she bore him not.

ION
And gave him as the picture represents?

CREUSA
Daughters of Cecrops these, charged not to see him.

ION
The virgins ope'd the interdicted chest?

CREUSA
And died, distaining with their blood the rock.

ION
But tell me, is this truth, or a vain rumour?

CREUSA
What wouldst thou ask? I am not scant of time.

ION
Thy sisters did Erechtheus sacrifice?

CREUSA
He slew the virgins, victims for their country.

ION
And thou of all thy sisters saved alone?

CREUSA
I was an infant in my mother's arms.

ION

And did the yawning earth swallow thy father?

CREUSA
By Neptune's trident smote; and so he perish'd.

ION
And Macrai call you not the fatal place?

CREUSA
Why dost thou ask? What thoughts hast thou recall'd?,

ION
Does Phoebus, do his lightnings honour it?

CREUSA
Honour! Why this? Would I had never seen it!

ION
Why? Dost thou hate the place dear to the god?

CREUSA
No: but for some base deed done in the cave.

ION
But what Athenian, lady, wedded thee?

CREUSA
Of Athens none, but one of foreign birth.

ION
What is his name? Noble he needs must be.

CREUSA
Xuthus, by Aeolus derived from Jove.

ION
How weds a stranger an Athenian born?

CREUSA
Euboea is a state neighbouring on Athens.

ION
A narrow sea flows, I have heard, between.

CREUSA
Joining the Athenian arms, that state he wasted.

ION

Confederate in the war, thence wedded thee?

CREUSA
The dowral meed of war, earn'd by his spear.

ION
Comest thou with him to Delphi, or alone?

CREUSA
With him, gone now to the Trophonian shrine.

ION
To view it, or consult the oracle?

CREUSA
Both that and this, anxious for one response.

ION
For the earth's fruits consult you, or for children?

CREUSA
Though wedded long, yet childless is our bed.

ION
Hast thou ne'er borne a child, that thou hast none?

CREUSA
My state devoid of children Phoebus knows.

ION
Bless'd in all else, luckless in this alone.

CREUSA
But who art thou? Bless'd I pronounce thy mother.

ION
Call'd as I am the servant of the god.

CREUSA
Presented by some state, or sold to this?

ION
I know not aught save this, I am the god's.

CREUSA
And in my turn, stranger, I pity thee.

ION

As knowing not my mother, or my lineage.

CREUSA
Hast thou thy dwelling here, or in some house?

ION
The temple is my house, ev'n when I sleep.

CREUSA
A child brought hither, or in riper years?

ION
An infant, as they say, who seem to know.

CREUSA
What Delphian dame sustain'd thee at her breast?

ION
I never knew a breast. She nourish'd me.

CREUSA
Who, hapless youth? Diseased, I find disease.

ION
The priestess: as a mother I esteem her.

CREUSA
Who to these manly years gave thee support?

ION
The altars, and the still-succeeding strangers.

CREUSA
Wretched, whoe'er she be, is she that bore thee.

ION
I to some woman am perchance a shame.

CREUSA
Are riches thine? Thou art well habited.

ION
Graced with these vestments by the god I serve.

CREUSA
Hast thou made no attempt to trace thy birth?

ION

I have no token, lady, for a proof.

CREUSA
Ah, like thy mother doth another suffer.

ION
Who? tell me: shouldst thou help me, what a joy

CREUSA
One for whose sake I come before my husband.

ION
Say for what end, that I may serve thee, lady.

CREUSA
To ask a secret answer of the god.

ION
Speak it: my service shall procure the rest.

CREUSA
Hear then the tale: but Modesty restrains me.

ION
Ah, let her not; her power avails not here.

CREUSA
My friend then says that to the embrace of Phoebus-

ION
A woman and a god! Say not so, stranger.

CREUSA
She bore a son: her father knew it not.

ION
Not so: a mortal's baseness he disdains.

CREUSA
This she affirms; and this, poor wretch, she suffer'd.

ION
What follow'd, if she knew the god's embrace?

CREUSA
The child, which hence had birth, she straight exposed.

ION

This exposed child, where is he? doth he live?

CREUSA
This no one knows; this wish I to inquire.

ION
If not alive, how probably destroyed?

CREUSA
Torn, she conjectures, by some beast of prey.

ION
What ground hath she on which to build that thought?

CREUSA
Returning to the place she found him not.

ION
Observed she drops of blood distain the path?

CREUSA
None, though with anxious heed she search'd around.

ION
What time hath pass'd since thus the child was lost?

CREUSA
Were he alive, his youth were such as thine.

ION
The god hath done him wrong: the unhappy mother-

CREUSA
Hath not to any child been mother since.

ION
What if in secret Phoebus nurtures him!

CREUSA
Unjust to enjoy alone a common right.

ION
Ah me! this cruel fate accords with mine.

CREUSA
For thee too thy unhappy mother mourns.

ION

Ah, melt me not to griefs I would forget!

CREUSA
I will be silent: but impart thy aid.

ION
Seest thou what most the inquiry will suppress?

CREUSA
And to my wretched friend what is not ill?

ION
How shall the god what he would hide reveal?

CREUSA
As placed on the oracular seat of Greece.

ION
The deed must cause him shame: convict him not.

CREUSA
To the poor sufferer 'tis the cause of grief.

ION
It cannot be; for who shall dare to give
The oracle? With justice would the god,
In his own dome affronted, pour on him
Severest vengeance, who should answer thee.
Desist then, lady: it becomes us ill,
In opposition to the god, to make
Inquiries at his shrine; by sacrifice
Before their altars, or the flight of birds,
Should we attempt to force the unwilling gods
To utter what they wish not, 'twere the excess
Of rudeness; what with violence we urge
'Gainst their consent would to no good avail us:
What their spontaneous grace confers on us,
That, lady, as a blessing we esteem.

LEADER OF THE CHORUS
How numberless the ills to mortal man,
And various in their form! One single blessing
By any one through life is scarcely found.

CREUSA
Nor here, nor there, O Phoebus, art thou just
To her; though absent, yet her words are present.
Nor didst thou save thy son, whom it became thee

To save; nor, though a prophet, wilt thou speak
To the sad mother who inquires of thee;
That, if he is no more, to him a tomb
May rise; but, if he lives, that he may bless
His mother's eyes. But even thus behooves us
To omit these things, if by the god denied
To know what most I wish.-But, for I see
The noble Xuthus this way bend, return'd
From the Trophonian cave; before my husband
Resume not, generous stranger, this discourse,
Lest it might cause me shame that thus I act
In secret, and perchance lead on to questions
I would not have explain'd. Our hapless sex
Oft feel our husbands' rigour: with the bad
The virtuous they confound, and treat us harshly.

[**XUTHUS** and his **RETINUE** enter.]

XUTHUS
With reverence to the god my first address
I pay: Hail, Phoebus! Lady, next to thee:
Absent so long, have I not caused thee fear?

CREUSA
Not much: as anxious thoughts 'gan rise, thou'rt come.

But, tell me, from Trophonius what reply
Bearest thou; what means whence offspring may arise?

XUTHUS
Unmeet he held it to anticipate
The answer of the god: one thing he told me.
That childless I should not return, nor thou,
Home from the oracle.

CREUSA
Goddess revered,
Mother of Phoebus, be our coming hither
In lucky hour; and our connubial bed
Be by thy son made happier than before!

XUTHUS
It shall be so. But who is president here?

ION
Without, that charge is mine; within, devolved
On others, stranger, seated near the tripod;
The chiefs of Delphi these, chosen by lot.

XUTHUS
'Tis well: all that I want is then complete.
Let me now enter: for the oracle
Is given, I hear, in common to all strangers
Before the shrine; on such a day, that falls
Propitious thus, the answer of the god
Would I receive: meanwhile, these laurel boughs
Bear round the altars; lady, breathe thy prayers
To every god, that from Apollo's shrine
I may bring back the promise of a son.

[**XUTHUS**, after giving the laurel boughs to **CREUSA**, enters the temple.]

CREUSA
It shall, it shall be so. Should Phoebus now
At least be willing to redress the fault
Of former times, he would not through the whole
Be friendly to us: yet will I accept
What he vouchsafes us, for he is a god.

[**CREUSA** departs to the shrines in the outer precinct of the temple.]

ION
Why does this stranger always thus revile
With obscure speech the god? Is it through love
Of her, for whom she asks? or to conceal
Some secret of importance? But to me
What is the daughter of Erechtheus? Naught
Concerns it me. Then let me to my task,
And sprinkle from the golden vase the dew.
Yet must I blame the god, if thus perforce
He mounts the bed of virgins, and by stealth
Becomes a father, leaving then his children
To die, regardless of them. Do not thou
Act thus; but, as thy power is great, respect
The virtues; for whoe'er, of mortal men,
Dares impious deeds, him the gods punish: how
Is it then just that you, who gave the laws
To mortals, should yourselves transgress those laws?,
If (though it is not thus, yet will I urge
The subject,)-if to mortals you shall pay
The penalty of forced embraces, thou,
Neptune, and Jove, that reigns supreme in heaven,
Will leave your temples treasureless by paying
The mulcts of your injustice: for unjust
You are, your pleasures to grave temperance
Preferring: and to men these deeds no more

Can it be just to charge as crimes, these deeds
If from the gods they imitate: on those
Who gave the ill examples falls the charge.

[**ION** goes out.]

CHORUS [singing, strophe]
Thee prompt to yield thy lenient aid,
And sooth a mother's pain:
And thee, my Pallas, martial maid,
I call: O, hear the strain!
Thou, whom the Titan from the head of Jove,
Prometheus, drew, bright Victory, come,
Descending from thy golden throne above;
Haste, goddess, to the Pythian dome,
Where Phoebus, from his central shrine,
Gives the oracle divine,
By the raving maid repeated,
On the hallow'd tripod seated:
O haste thee, goddess, and with thee
The daughter of Latona bring;
A virgin thou, a virgin she,
Sisters to the Delphian king;
Him, virgins, let your vows implore,
That now his pure oracular power
Will to Erechtheus' ancient line declare
The blessing of a long-expected heir!

[antistrophe]

To mortal man this promised grace
Sublimest pleasure brings,
When round the father's hearth a race
In blooming lustre springs.
The wealth, the honours, from their high-drawn line
From sire to son transmitted down,
Shall with fresh glory through their offspring shine,
And brighten with increased renown:
A guard, when ills begin to lower,
Dear in fortune's happier hour;
For their country's safety waking,
Firm in fight the strong spear shaking;
More than proud wealth's exhaustless store,
More than a monarch's bride to reign,
The dear delight, to virtue's lore
Careful the infant mind to train.
Doth any praise the childless state?
The joyless, loveless life I hate;

No; my desires to moderate wealth I bound,
But let me see my children smile around.

[epode]

Ye rustic seats, Pan's dear delight;
Ye caves of Macrai's rocky height,
Where oft the social virgins meet,
And weave the dance with nimble feet;
Descendants from Aglauros they
In the third line, with festive play,
Minerva's hallow'd fane before
The verdant plain light-tripping o'er,
When thy pipe's quick-varying sound
Rings, O Pan, these caves around;
Where, by Apollo's love betray'd,
Her child some hapless mother laid,
Exposed to each night-prowling beast,
Or to the ravenous birds a feast;
For never have I heard it told,
Nor wrought it in historic gold,
That happiness attends the race,
When gods with mortals mix the embrace.

[**ION** re-enters.]

ION
Ye female train, that place yourselves around
This incense-breathing temple's base, your lord
Awaiting, hath he left the sacred tripod
And oracle, or stays he in the shrine,
Making inquiries of his childless state?

LEADER OF THE CHORUS
Yet in the temple, stranger, he remains.

ION
But he comes forth; the sounding doors announce
His near approach; behold, our lord is here.

[**XUTHUS** enters from the temple. He rushes to greet **ION**.]

XUTHUS
Health to my son! This first address is proper.

ION
I have my health: be in thy senses thou,
And both are well.

XUTHUS
O let me kiss thy hand,
And throw mine arms around thee.

ION
Art thou, stranger,
Well in thy wits? or hath the god's displeasure
Bereft thee of thy reason?

XUTHUS
Reason bids,
That which is dearest being found, to wish
A fond embrace.

ION
Off, touch me not; thy hands
Will mar the garlands of the god.

XUTHUS
My touch
Asserts no pledge: my own, and that most dear,
I find.

ION
Wilt thou not keep thee distant, ere
Thou hast my arrow in thy heart?

XUTHUS
Why fly me,
When thou shouldst own what is most fond of thee?

ION
I am not fond of curing wayward strangers,
And madmen.

XUTHUS
Kill me, raise my funeral pyre;
But, if thou kill me, thou wilt kill thy father.

ION
My father thou! how so? it makes me laugh
To hear thee.

XUTHUS
This my words may soon explain.

ION

What wilt thou say to me?

XUTHUS
I am thy father,
And thou my son.

ION
Who declares this?

XUTHUS
The god,
That nurtured thee, though mine.

ION
Thou to thyself
Art witness.

XUTHUS
By the oracle inform'd.

ION
Misled by some dark answer.

XUTHUS
Well I heard it.

ION
What were the words of Phoebus?

XUTHUS
That who first
Should meet me-

ION
How?—what meeting?

XUTHUS
As I pass'd.
Forth from the temple.

ION
What the event to him?

XUTHUS
He is my son.

ION
Born so, or by some other

Presented?

XUTHUS
Though a present, born my son.

ION
And didst thou first meet me?

XUTHUS
None else, my son.

ION
This fortune whence?

XUTHUS
At that we marvel both.

ION
Who is my mother?

XUTHUS
That I cannot say.

ION
Did not the god inform thee?

XUTHUS
Through my joy,
For this I ask'd not.

ION
Haply from the earth
I sprung, my mother.

XUTHUS
No, the earth no sons
Produces.

ION
How then am I thine?

XUTHUS
I know not.
To Phoebus I appeal.

ION
Be this discourse
Chang'd to some other.

XUTHUS
This delights me most.

ION
Hast thou e'er mounted an unlawful bed?

XUTHUS
In foolishness of youth.

ION
Was that before
Thy marriage with the daughter of Erechtheus?

XUTHUS
Since never.

ION
Owe I then my birth to that?

XUTHUS
The time agrees.

ION
How came I hither then?

XUTHUS
I can form no conjecture.

ION
Was I brought
From some far distant part?

XUTHUS
That fills my mind
With doubtful musing.

ION
Didst thou e'er before
Visit the Pythian rock?

XUTHUS
Once, at the feast
Of Bacchus.

ION
By some public host received?

XUTHUS
Who with the Delphian damsels-

ION
To the orgies
Led thee, or how?

XUTHUS
And with the Maenades
Of Bacchus-

ION
In the temperate hour, or warm
With wine?

XUTHUS
Amid the revels of the god.

ION
From thence I date my birth.

XUTHUS
And fate, my son,
Hath found thee.

ION
How then came I to the temple?

XUTHUS
Perchance exposed.

ION
The state of servitude
Have I escaped.

XUTHUS
Thy father now, my son,
Receive.

ION
Indecent were it in the god
Not to confide.

XUTHUS
Thy thoughts are just.

ION
What else

Would we?

XUTHUS
Thou seest what thou oughtst to see.

ION
Am I the son then of the son of Jove?

XUTHUS
Such is thy fortune.

ION
Those that gave me birth
Do I embrace?

XUTHUS
Obedient to the god.

ION
My father, hail!

XUTHUS
That dear name I accept
With joy.

ION
This present day-

XUTHUS
Hath made me happy.

ION
O my dear mother, when shall I behold
Thy face? Whoe'er thou art, more wish I now
To see thee than before; but thou perchance
Art dead, and nothing our desires avail.

LEADER OF THE CHORUS
We in the blessing of our house rejoice.
Yet wish we that our mistress too were happy
In children, and the lineage of Erechtheus.

XUTHUS
Well hath the god accomplish'd this, my son,
Discovering thee, well hath he joined thee to me;
And thou hast found the most endearing ties,
To which, before this hour, thou wast a stranger.
And the warm wish, which thou hast well conceived,

Is likewise mine, that thou mayst find thy mother;
I from what woman thou derivest thy birth.
This, left to time, may haply be discover'd.
Now quit this hallow'd earth, the god no more
Attending, and to mine accord thy mind,
To visit Athens, where thy father's sceptre,
No mean one, waits thee, and abundant wealth:
Nor, though thou grieve one parent yet unknown,
Shalt thou be censured as ignobly born,
Or poor: no, thou art noble, and thy state
Adorn'd with rich possessions. Thou art silent.
Why is thine eye thus fixed upon the ground?
Why on thy brow that cloud? The smile of joy
Vanish'd, thou strikest thy father's heart with fear.

ION
Far other things appear when nigh, than seen
At distance. I indeed embrace my fortune,
In thee my father found. But hear what now
Wakes sad reflections. Proud of their high race
Are your Athenians, natives of the land,
Not drawn from foreign lineage: I to them
Shall come unwelcome, in two points defective,
My father not a native, and myself
Of spurious birth: loaded with this reproach,
If destitute of power, I shall be held
Abject and worthless: should I rush among
The highest order of the state, and wish
To appear important, inferior ranks
Will hate me; aught above them gives disgust.
The good, the wise, men form'd to serve the state,
Are silent, nor at public honours aim
Too hastily: by such, were I not quiet
In such a bustling state, I should be deem'd
Ridiculous, and proverb'd for a fool.
Should I attain the dignity of those,
Whose approved worth hath raised them to the height
Of public honours, by such suffrage more
Should I be watch'd; for they that hold in states
Rule and pre-eminence, bear hostile minds
To all that vie with them. And should I come
To a strange house a stranger, to a woman
Childless herself, who that misfortune shared
Before with thee, now sees it her sole lot,
And feels it bitterly, would she not hate me,
And that with justice? When I stand before them.
With what an eye would she, who hath no child,
Look on thy child? In tenderness to her,

Thy wife, thou must forsake me, or embroil
Thy house in discord, if thou favour me.
What murderous means, what poisonous drugs for men
Have women with inventive rage prepared!
Besides, I have much pity for thy wife,
Now growing old without a child, that grief
Unmerited, the last of her high race,
The exterior face indeed of royalty,
So causelessly commended, bath its brightness;
Within, all gloom: for what sweet peace of mind,
What happiness is his, whose years are pass'd
In comfortless suspicion, and the dread
Of violence? Be mine the humble blessings
Of private life, rather than be a king,
From the flagitious forced to choose my friends,
And hate the virtuous through the fear of death.
Gold, thou mayst tell me, hath o'er things like these
A sovereign power, and riches give delight:
I have no pleasure in this noisy pomp,
Nor, while I guard my riches, in the toil:
Be mine a modest mean that knows not care.
And now, my father, hear the happy state
I here enjoy'd; and first, to mortal man
That dearest blessing, leisure, and no bustle
To cause disturbance: me no ruffian force
Shoved from the way: it is not to be borne,
When every insolent and worthless wretch
Makes you give place. The worship of the god
Employ'd my life, or (no unpleasing task)
Service to men well pleased: the parting guest
I bade farewell-welcomed the new-arrived.
Thus something always new made every hour
Glide sweetly on; and to the human mind
That dearest wish, though some regard it not,
To be, what duty and my nature made me,
Just to the god: revolving this, my father,
I wish not for thy Athens to exchange
This state; permit me to myself to live;
Dear to the mind pleasures that arise
From humble life, as those which greatness brings.

LEADER OF THE CHORUS
Well hast thou said, if those whom my soul holds
Most dear shall in thy words find happiness.

XUTHUS
No more of this discourse; learn to be happy.
It is my will that thou begin it here,

Where first I found thee, son: a general feast
Will I provide, and make a sacrifice,
Which at thy birth I made not: at my table
Will I receive thee as a welcome guest,
And cheer thee with the banquet, then conduct the
To Athens with me as a visitant,
Not as my son: for, mid my happiness,
I would not grieve my wife, who hath no child.

ION
But I will watch the occasions time may bring,
And so present thee, and obtain her leave
That thou mayst hold the sceptre which I bear.
Ion I name thee, as befits thy fortune,
As first thou met'st me from the hallow'd shrine
As I came forth; assemble then thy friends,
Invite them all to share the joyful feast,
Since thou art soon to leave the Delphic state.
And you, ye females, keep, I charge you, keep
This secret; she that tells my wife shall die.

ION
Let us then go; yet one thing to my fortune
Is wanting: if I find not her that bore me,
Life hath no joy. Might I indulge a wish,
It were to find her an Athenian dame,
That from my mother I might dare to assume
Some confidence; for he whose fortune leads him
To a free state proud of their unmix'd race,
Though call'd a citizen, must close his lips
With servile awe, for freedom is not his.

[**XUTHUS** and **ION** go out.]

CHORUS [singing, strophe]
Yes, sisters, yes, the streaming eye,
The swelling heart I see, the bursting sigh,
When thus rejoicing in his son
Our queen her royal lord shall find,
And give to grief her anguish'd mind,
Afflicted, childless, and alone.
What means this voice divine,
Son of Latona, fate-declaring power?
Whence is this youth, so fondly graced,
That to ripe manhood, from his infant hour,
Hath in thy hallow'd courts been plac'd
And nurtured at thy shrine?
Thy dark reply delights not me;

Lurking beneath close fraud I see:
Where will this end? I fear, I fear-
'Tis strange, and strange events must hence ensue:
But grateful sounds it to his ear,
The youth, that in another's state
(Who sees not that my words are true?)
Enjoys the fraud, and triumphs in his fate.

[antistrophe]

Say, sisters, say, with duteous zeal
Shall we this secret to our queen reveal?
She, to her royal lord resign'd,
With equal hope, wlth equal care,
Form'd her his joys, his griefs to share,
And gave him an her willing mind.
But joys are his alone;
While she, poor mourner, with a weight of woes,
To hoary age advancing, bends;
He the bright smile of prosperous fortune knows.
Ev'n thus, unhonour'd by his friends,
Plac'd on another's throne,
Mischance and ruin on him wait,
Who fails to guard its happy state.
Him may mischance and ruin seize,
Who round my lov'd queen spreads his wily trains.
No god may his oblation please,
No favouring flame to him ascend!
To her my faith, my zeal remains,
Known to her ancient royal house a friend.

[epode]

Now the father and the new-found son
The festive table haste to spread,
Where to the skies Parnassus lifts his head,
And deep beneath the hanging stone
Forms in its rudely-rifted side
A cavern wild and wide;
Where Bacchus, shaking high his midnight flames,
In many a light fantastic round
Dances o'er the craggy ground,
And revels with his frantic dames.
Ne'er to my city let him come,
This youth: no, rather let him die,
And sink into an early tomb!
With an indignant eye
Athens would view the stranger's pride

Within her gates triumphant ride:
Enough for her the honour'd race that springs
From old Erechtheus and her line of kings.

[**CREUSA** and her aged **TUTOR** enter.]

CREUSA
Thou venerable man, whose guiding voice
My father, while he lived, revered, advance
Up to the oracular seat thy aged steps;
That, if the royal Phoebus should pronounce
Promise of offspring, thou with me mayst share
The joy; for pleasing is it when with friends
Good fortune we receive; if aught of ill
(Avert it, Heaven!) befalls, a friend's kind eye
Beams comfort; thee, as once thou didst revere
My father, though thy queen, I now revere.

TUTOR
In thee, my child, the nobleness of manners
Which graced thy royal ancestors yet lives;
Thou never wilt disgrace thy high-born lineage.
Lead me, then, lead me to the shrine, support me:
High is the oracular seat, and steep the ascent;
Be thou assistant to the foot of age.

CREUSA
Follow; be heedful where thou set thy steps.

TUTOR
I am: my foot is slow, my heart hath wings.

CREUSA
Fix thy staff firm on this loose-rolling ground.

TUTOR
That hath no eyes; and dim indeed my sight.

CREUSA
Well hast thou said; on cheerful then, and faint not.

TUTOR
I have the will, but o'er constraint no power.

CREUSA
Ye females, on my richly-broider'd works
Faithful attendants, say, respecting children,
For which we came, what fortune hath my lord

Borne hence? if good, declare it: you shall find
That to no thankless masters you give joy.

LEADER OF THE CHORUS
O fortune!

CREUSA
To thy speech this is a proem
Not tuned to happiness.

LEADER OF THE CHORUS
Unhappy fortune!
But why distress me for the oracle
Given to our lords? Be that as fate requires
In things which threaten death, what shall we do?

CREUSA
What means this strain of woe? Whence are these fears?

LEADER OF THE CHORUS
What! shall we speak, or bury this in silence?

CREUSA
Speak, though thy words bring wretchedness to me.

LEADER OF THE CHORUS
It shall be spoken, were I twice to die.
To thee, my queen, it is not given to clasp
In thy fond arms a child, or at thy breast
To hold it.

TUTOR
O my child, would I were dead!

CREUSA
Yes, this is wretchedness indeed, a grief
That makes life joyless.

TUTOR
This is ruin to us.

CREUSA
Unhappy me! this is a piercing grief,
That rends my heart with anguish.

TUTOR
Groan not yet.

CREUSA
Yet is the affliction present.

TUTOR
Till we learn-

CREUSA
To me what tidings?

TUTOR
If a common fate
Await our lord, partaker of thy griefs,
Or thou alone art thus unfortunate.

LEADER OF THE CHORUS
To him, old man, the god hath given a son,
And happiness is his unknown to her.

CREUSA
To ill this adds the deepest ill, a grief
For me to mourn.

TUTOR
Born of some other woman
Is this child yet to come, or did the god
Declare one now in being?

LEADER OF THE CHORUS
One advanced
To manhood's prime he gave him: I was present.

CREUSA
What hast thou said? Thy words denounce to me
Sorrows past speech, past utterance.

TUTOR
And to me.

CREUSA
How was this oracle accomplish'd? Tell me
With clearest circumstance: who is this youth?

LEADER OF THE CHORUS
Him as a son Apollo gave, whom first,
Departing from the god, thy lord should meet.

CREUSA
O my unhappy fate! I then am left

Childless to pass my life, childless, alone,
Amid my lonely house! Who was declared?
Whom did the husband of this wretch first meet?
How meet him? Where behold him? Tell me all.

LEADER OF THE CHORUS
Dost thou, my honoured mistress, call to mind
The youth that swept the temple? This is he.

CREUSA
O, through the liquid air that I could fly,
Far from the land of Greece, ev'n to the stars
Fix'd in the western sky! Ah me, what grief,
What piercing grief is mine I

TUTOR
Say, by what name
Did he address his son, if thou hast heard it?
Or does it rest in silence, yet unknown?

LEADER OF THE CHORUS
Ion, for that he first advanced to meet him.

TUTOR
And of what mother?

LEADER OF THE CHORUS
That I could not learn:
Abrupt was his departure (to inform thee
Of all I know, old man) to sacrifice,
With hospitable rites, a birthday feast;
And in the hallow'd cave, from her apart,
With his new son to share the common banquet.

TUTOR
Lady, we by thy husband are betrayed,
For I with thee am grieved, with contrived fraud
Insulted, from thy father's house cast forth.
I speak not this in hatred to thy lord,
But that I love thee more: a stranger he
Came to the city and thy royal house,
And wedded thee, all thy inheritance
Receiving, by some other woman now
Discover'd to have children privately:
How privately I'll tell thee: when he saw
Thou hadst no child, it pleased him not to bear
A fate like thine; but by some favourite slave,
His paramour by stealth, he hath a son.

Him to some Delphian gave he, distant far,
To educate; who to this sacred house
Consign'd, as secret here, received his nurture.
He knowing this, and that his son advanced
To manhood, urged thee to attend him hither,
Pleading thy childless state. Nor hath the god
Deceived thee: he deceived thee, and long since
Contrived this wily plan to rear his son,
That, if convicted, he might charge the god,
Himself excusing: should the fraud succeed,
He would observe the times when he might safely
Consign to him the empire of thy land.
And this new name was at his leisure form'd,
Ion, for that he came by chance to meet him.
I hate those ill-designing men, that form
Plans of injustice, and then gild them over
With artificial ornament: to me
Far dearer is the honest simple friend,
Than one whose quicker wit is train'd to ill.
And to complete this fraud, thou shalt be urged
To take into thy house, to lord it there,
This low-born youth, this offspring of a slave.
Though ill, it had been open, had he pleaded
Thy want of children, and, thy leave obtain'd,
Brought to thy house a son that could have boasted
His mother noble; or, if that displeased thee,
He might have sought a wife from Aeolus.
Behooves thee then to act a woman's part,
Or grasp the sword, or drug the poison'd bowl,
Or plan some deep design to kill thy husband,
And this his son, before thou find thy death
From them: if thou delay, thy life is lost:
For when beneath one roof two foes are met,
The one must perish. I with ready zeal
Will aid thee in this work, and kill the youth,
Entering the grot where he prepares the feast;
Indifferent in my choice, so that I pay
What to my lords I owe, to live or die.
If there is aught that causes slaves to blush,
It is the name; in all else than the free
The slave is nothing worse, if he be virtuous.
I too, my honour'd queen, with cheerful mind
Will share thy fate, or die, or live with honour.

CREUSA [chanting]
How, o my soul, shall I be silent, how
Disclose this secret? Can I bid farewell
To modesty? What else restrains my tongue?

To how severe a trial am I brought!
Hath not my husband wrong'd me? Of my house
I am deprived, deprived of children; hope
Is vanish'd, which my heart could not resign,
With many an honest wish this furtive bed
Concealing, this lamented bed concealing.
But by the star-bespangled throne of Jove,
And by the goddess high above my rocks
Enshrined, by the moist banks that bend around
The hallow'd lake by Triton form'd, no longer
Will I conceal this bed, but ease my breast,
The oppressive load discharged. Mine eyes drop tears,
My soul is rent, to wretchedness ensnared
By men, by gods, whom I will now disclose,
Unkind betrayers of the beds they forced.
O thou, that wakest on thy seven-string'd lyre
Sweet notes, that from the rustic lifeless horn
Enchant the ear with heavenly melody,
Son of Latona, thee before this light
Will I reprove. Thou camest to me, with gold
Thy locks all glittering, as the vermeil flowers
I gather'd in my vest to deck my bosom
With the spring's glowing hues; in my white hand
Thy hand enlocking, to the cavern'd rock
Thou led'st me; naught avail'd my cries, that call'd
My mother; on thou led'st me, wanton god,
Immodestly, to Venus paying homage.
A son I bare thee, O my wretched fate!
Him (for I fear'd my mother) in thy cave
I placed, where I unhappy was undone
By thy unhappy love. Woe, woe is me!
And now my son and thine, ill-fated babe,
Is rent by ravenous vultures; thou, meanwhile,
Art to thy lyre attuning strains of joy.
Set of Latona, thee I call aloud
Who from thy golden seat, thy central throne,
Utterest thine oracle: my voice shall reach
Thine ear: ungrateful lover, to my husband,
No grace requiting, thou hast given a son
To bless his house; my son and thine, unown'd,
Perish'd a prey to birds; the robes that wrapp'd
The infant's limbs, his mother's work, lost with him.
Delos abhors thee, and the laurel boughs
With the soft foliage of the palm o'erhung,
Grasping whose round trunk with her hands divine,
Latona thee, her hallow'd offspring, bore.

LEADER OF THE CHORUS

Ah, what a mighty treasury of ills
Is open'd here, a copious source of tears!

TUTOR
Never, my daughter, can I sate my eyes
With looking on thy face: astonishment
Bears me beyond my senses. I had stemm'd
One tide of evils, when another flood
High-surging overwhelm'd me from the words
Which thou hast utter'd, from the present ills
To an ill train of other woes transferr'd.
What say'st thou? Of what charge dost thou implead
The god? What son hast thou brought forth? Where placed him
A feast for vultures? Tell me all again.

CREUSA
Though I must blush, old man, yet I will speak.

TUTOR
I mourn with generous grief at a friend's woes.

CREUSA
Hear then: the northward-pointing cave thou knowest,

And the Cecropian rocks, which we call Macrai.

TUTOR
Where stands a shrine to Pan, and altars nigh.

CREUSA
There in a dreadful conflict I engaged.

TUTOR
What! my tears rise ready to meet thy words.

CREUSA
By Phoebus drawn reluctant to his bed.

TUTOR
Was this, my daughter, such as I suppose?

CREUSA
I know not: but if truth, I will confess it.

TUTOR
Didst thou in silence mourn this secret ill?

CREUSA

This was the grief I now disclose to thee.

TUTOR
This love of Phoebus how didst thou conceal?

CREUSA
I bore a son. Hear me, old man, with patience.

TUTOR
Where? who assisted? or wast thou alone?

CREUSA
Alone, in the same cave where compress'd.

TUTOR
Where is thy son, that childless now no more

CREUSA
Dead, good old man, to beasts of prey exposed.

TUTOR
Dead! and the ungrateful Phoebus gives no aid?

CREUSA
None: in the house of Pluto a young guest.

TUTOR
Whose hands exposed him? Surely not thine own.

CREUSA
Mine, in the shades of night, wrapp'd in his vests.

TUTOR
Hadst thou none with thee conscious to this deed?

CREUSA
My misery, and the secret place alone.

TUTOR
How durst thou in a cavern leave thy son?

CREUSA
How? uttering many sad and plaintive words.

TUTOR
Ah, cruel was thy deed, the god more cruel.

CREUSA

Hadst thou but seen him stretch his little hands!

TUTOR
Seeking the breast, or reaching to thine arms?

CREUSA
To this, deprived of which he suffer'd wrong.

TUTOR
And what induced thee to expose thy child?

CREUSA
Hope that the god's kind care would save his son.

TUTOR
How are the glories of thy house destroy'd!

CREUSA
Why, thine head cover'd, dost thou pour these tears?

TUTOR
To see thee and thy father thus unhappy.

CREUSA
This is the state of man: nothing stands firm.

TUTOR
No longer then, my child, let grief oppress us.

CREUSA
What should I do? In misery all is doubt.

TUTOR
First on the god that wrong'd thee be avenged.

CREUSA
How shall a mortal 'gainst a god prevail?

TUTOR
Set this revered oracular shrine on fire.

CREUSA
I fear: ev'n now I have enough of ills.

TUTOR
Attempt what may be done then; kill thy husband.

CREUSA

The nuptial bed I reverence, and his goodness.

TUTOR
This son then, which is now brought forth against thee.

CREUSA
How? Could that be, how warmly should I wish it.

TUTOR
Thy train hath swords: instruct them to the deed.

CREUSA
I go with speed: but where shall it be done?

TUTOR
In the hallow'd tent, where now he feasts his friends.

CREUSA
An open murder, and with coward slaves!

TUTOR
If mine displease, propose thou some design.

CREUSA
I have it, close and easy to achieve.

TUTOR
In both my faithful services are thine.

CREUSA
Hear then: not strange to thee the giants' war.

TUTOR
When they in Phlegra fought against the gods.

CREUSA
There the earth brought forth the Gorgon, horrid monster.

TUTOR
In succour of her sons to annoy the gods?

CREUSA
Ev'n so: her Pallas slew, daughter of Jove.

TUTOR
What fierce and dreadful form did she then wear?

CREUSA

Her breastplate arm'd with vipers wreathed around.

TUTOR
A well-known story; often have I heard it.

CREUSA
Her spoils before her breast Minerva wore.

TUTOR
The aegis; so they call the vest of Pallas.

CREUSA
So named, when in the war she join'd the gods.

TUTOR
But how can this, my child, annoy thy foes?

CREUSA
Thou canst not but remember Erichthonius.

TUTOR
Whom first of thy high race the earth brought forth.

CREUSA
To him while yet an infant Pallas gave-

TUTOR
What? Thy slow preface raises expectation.

CREUSA
Two drops of blood that from the Gorgon fell.

TUTOR
And on the human frame what power have these?

CREUSA
The one works death, the other heals disease.

TUTOR
In what around the infant's body hung?

CREUSA
Enclosed in gold: he gave them to my father.

TUTOR
At his decease then they devolved to thee?

CREUSA

Ay, and I wear it as a bracelet; look.

TUTOR
Their double qualities how temper'd, say.

CREUSA
This drop, which from her hollow vein distill'd,-

TUTOR
To what effect applied? What is its power?

CREUSA
Medicinal, of sovereign use to life.

TUTOR
The other drop, what faculties hath that?

CREUSA
It kills, the poison of the Gorgon dragons.

TUTOR
And dost thou bear this gore blended in one?

CREUSA
No, separate; for with ill good mixes not.

TUTOR
O my dear child, thou hast whate'er we want.

CREUSA
With this the boy shall die, and thou shalt kill him.

TUTOR
Where? How? 'Tis thine to speak, to dare be mine.

CREUSA
At Athens, when he comes beneath my roof.

TUTOR
I like not this; what I proposed displeased.

CREUSA
Dost thou surmise what enters now my thoughts?

TUTOR
Suspicion waits thee, though thou kill him not.

CREUSA

Thou hast judged well: a stepdame's hate is proverb'd.

TUTOR
Then kill him here; thou mayst disown the deed.

CREUSA
My mind ev'n now anticipates the pleasure.

TUTOR
Thus shalt thou meet thy husband's wiles with wiles

CREUSA
This shalt thou do: this little golden casket
Take from my hand, Minerva's gift of old;
To where my husband secretly prepares
The sacrifice, bear this beneath thy vest.
That supper ended, when they are to pour
Libations to the gods, thou mayst infuse
In the youth's goblet this: but take good heed,
Let none observe thee; drug his cup alone
Who thinks to lord it in my house: if once
It pass his lips, his foot shall never reach
Illustrious Athens: death awaits him here.

[She gives him the casket.]

TUTOR
Go thou then to the hospitable house
Prepared for thy reception: be it mine,
Obedient to thy word to do this deed.
Come then, my aged foot, be once more young
In act, though not in years, for past recall
That time is fled: kill him, and bear him forth.
Well may the prosperous harbour virtuous thought;
But when thou wouldst avenge thee on thy foes,
There is no law of weight to hinder thee.

[They both go out.]

CHORUS [singing, strophe 1]
Daughter of Ceres, Trivia hear,
Propitious regent of each public way
Amid the brightness of the day,
Nor less when night's dark hour engenders fear;
The fulness of this goblet guide
To check with death this stripling's pride,
For whom my queen this fatal draught prepares,
Tinged with the Gorgon's venom'd gore:

That seat, which mid Erechtheus' royal heirs
His pride claims, it shall claim no more:
Never may one of alien blood disgrace
The imperial honours of that high-born race!

[antistrophe 1]

Should not this work of fate succeed,
Nor the just vengeance of my queen prevail;
Should this apt time of daring fail,
And hope, that flatters now, desert the deed;
Slaughter shall other means afford,
The strangling cord, the piercing sword;
For rage from disappointed rage shall flow,
And try each. various form of death;
For never shall my queen this torment know;
Ne'er while she draws this vital breath,
Brook in her house that foreign lords should shine,
Clothed with the splendours of her ancient line.

[strophe 2]

Thou whom the various hymn delights,
Then thy bright choir of beauteous dames among,
Dancing the stream's soft brink along,
Thou seest the guardian of thy mystic rites,
Thy torch its midnight vigils keep,
Thine eye meantime disdaining sleep;
While with thee dances Jove's star-spangled plain.
And the moon dances up the sky:
Ye nymphs, that lead to grots your frolic train,
Beneath the gulfy founts that lie:
Thou gold-crown'd queen, through night's dark regions fear'd,

And thou, her mother, power revered,
How should I blush to see this youth unknown!
This Delphic vagrant, hope to seize the throne.

[antistrophe 2]

You, who the melting soul to move,
In loose, dishonest airs the Muse employ
To celebrate love's wanton joy,
The joy of unallow'd, unholy love,
See how our pure and modest law
Can lavish man's lewd deeds o'erawe!
Ye shameless bards, revoke each wanton air;
No more these melting measures frame;

Bid the chaste muse in Virtue's cause declare,
And mark man's lawless bed with shame!
Ungrateful is this Jove-descended lord;
For, his wife's childless bed abhorr'd,
Lewdly he courts the embrace of other dames,
And with a spurious son his pride inflames.

[An **ATTENDANT of CREUSA** enters.]

ATTENDANT
Athenian dames, where shall I find our queen,
The daughter of Erechtheus? Seeking her,
This city have I walked around in vain.

LEADER OF THE CHORUS
And for what cause, my fellow-slave? What means
Thy hasty foot? What tidings dost thou bring?

ATTENDANT
We are discover'd; and the rulers here
Seek her, that she may die o'erwhelm'd with stones.

LEADER OF THE CHORUS
Ah me! what wouldst thou say? Are our designs
Of secret ruin to this youth disclosed?

ATTENDANT
They are; and know, the worst of ills await you.

LEADER OF THE CHORUS
How were our dark devices brought to light?

ATTENDANT
The god, that justice might receive no stain
Caused it to triumph o'er defeated wrong.

LEADER OF THE CHORUS
How? as a suppliant, I conjure thee, tell me
Of this inform'd, if we must die, more freely
Wish we to die than see the light of heaven.

ATTENDANT
Soon as the husband of Creusa left
The god's oracular shrine, this new-found son
He to the feast, and sacrifice prepared
To the high gods, led with him. Xuthus then
Went where the hallow'd flame of Bacchus mounts,
That on each rock's high point the victim's blood

Might flow, a grateful offering for his son
Thus recognised, to whom he gave in charge,
"Stay thou, and with the artist's expert aid
Erect the sheltering tent: my rites perform'd
To the kind gods that o'er the genial bed
Preside, should I be there detain'd too long,
Spread the rich table to my present friends."
This said, he led the victims to the rocks.
Meanwhile with reverent heed the son 'gan rear
On firm supporters the wide tent, whose sides
No masonry require, yet framed to exclude
The mid-day sun's hot beams, or his last rays
When sinking in the west: the lengthen'd lines
Equally distant comprehend a square
Of twice five thousand feet (the skilful thus
Compute it), space to feast (for so he will'd)
All Delphi: from the treasures of the god
He took the sacred tapestry, and around
Hung the rich shade, on which the admiring eye
Gazes with fix'd delight: first over head,
Like a broad pennon spread the extended woof,
Which from the Amazonian spoils the son
Of Jove, Alcides, hallow'd to the god;
In its bright texture interwov'n a sky
Gathering the stars in its ethereal round,
While downwards to the western wave the sun
His steeds declines, and to his station high
Draws up the radiant flame of Hesperus.
Meanwhile the Night robed in her sable stole,
Her unreign'd car advances; on her state
The stars attend; the Pleiads mounting high,
And with his glittering sword Orion arm'd;
Above, Arcturus to the golden pole
Inclines; full-orb'd the month-dividing moon
Takes her bright station, and the Hyades
Marked by the sailor: distant in the rear,
Aurora ready to relume the day,
And put the stars to flight. The sides were graced
With various textures of the historic woof,
Barbaric arguments; in gallant trim
Against the fleet of Greece the hostile fleet
Rides proudly on. Here monstrous forms portray'd
Human and brutal mix'd: the Thracian steeds
Are seized, the hinds, and the adventurous chase
Of savage lions: figured nigh the doors,
Cecrops, attended by his daughter's, roll'd
His serpent train: in the ample space within
He spread the festal table, richly deck'd

With golden goblets. Now the herald walk'd
His round, each native that inclined to grace
The feast inviting: to the crowded tent
They hasten, crown'd with garlands, and partake
The exquisite repast. The pleasured sense
Now satiate, in the midst an old man stood,
Officious in his ministry, which raised
Much mirth among the guests; for from the urns
He fill'd the lavers, and with fragrant myrrh
Incensed the place; the golden bowls he claim'd
His charge. When now the jocund pipes 'gan breathe
Harmonious airs, and the fresh goblet stood
Ready to walk its round, the old man said,
"Away with these penurious cups, and bring
Capacious bowls; so shall you quickly bathe
Your spirits in delight." With speed were brought
Goblets of gold and silver: one he took
Of choicer frame; and, seemingly intent
To do his young lord honour, the full vase
Gave to his hands, but in the wine infused
A drug of poisonous power, which, it is said,
His queen supplied, that the new son no more
Might view the light of heav'n; but unobserved
He mix'd it. As the youth among the rest
Pour'd the libation, 'mid the attendant slaves
Words of reproach one utter'd: he, as train'd
Within the temple and with expert seers,
Deem'd them of evil omen, and required
Another goblet to be filled afresh-
The former a libation to the god,
He cast upon the ground, instructing all
To pour, like him, the untasted liquor down.
Silence ensued: the sacred bowls we fill
With wines of Byblos; when a troop of doves
Came fluttering in, for undisturb'd they haunt
The dome of Phoebus: in the floating wine
They dipp'd their bills to drink, then raised their heads,

Gurgling it down their beauteous-plumed throats.
Harmless to all the spilt wine, save to her
That lighted where the youth had pour'd his bowl:
She drank, and straight convulsive shiverings seized
Her beauteous plumes; around in giddy rings
She whirl'd, and in a strange and mournful note
Seem'd to lament: amazement seized the guests,
Seeing the poor bird's pangs: her heart heaved thick,
And stretching out her scarlet legs, she died.
Rending his robes, the son of Phoebus given

Sprung from the table, and aloud exclaim'd,-
"What wretch design'd to kill me? Speak, old man:
Officious was thy ministry; the bowl
I from thy hand received." Then straight he seized
His aged arm, and to the question held him,
As in the fact discover'd: he thus caught,
Reluctant and constrain'd, own'd the bold deed,
The deadly goblet by Creusa drugg'd.
Forth from the tent, the guests attending, rush'd
The youth announced by Phoebus, and amid
The Pythian regents says,-"O hallow'd land!
This stranger dame, this daughter of Erechtheus
Attempts my life by poison." Then decreed
The Delphian lords (nor did one voice dissent)
That she should die, my mistress, from the rock
Cast headlong, as the deed was aim'd against
A sacred life, and impiously presumed
This hallow'd place with murder to profane.
Demanded by the state, she this way bends
Her wretched steps. Unhappy to this shrine
She came through fond desire of children; here,
Together with her hopes, her life is lost.

CHORUS [singing]
None, there is none, from death no flight,
To me no refuge; our dark deed
Betray'd, betray'd to open light;
The festive bowl, with sprightly wine that flow'd
Mix'd with the Gorgon's viperous blood,
An offering to the dead decreed,
All is betray'd to light: and I,
Cast headlong from the rock, must die.
What flight shall save me from this death,
Borne on swift pinions through the air,
Sunk to the darksome cave beneath,
Or mounted on the rapid car?
Or shall the flying bark unfurl its sails?
Alas, my queen, no flight avails,
Save when some god's auspicious power
Shall snatch us from the dangerous hour.
Unhappy queen, what pangs shall rend thy heart!
Shall we, who plann'd the deathful deed,
Be caught within the toils we spread,
While justice claims severe her chast'ning part?

[**CREUSA** rushes in.]

CREUSA

I am pursued, ye faithful females, doom'd
To death: the Pythian council hath decreed it:
My life is forfeited.

LEADER OF THE CHORUS
Unhappy lady,
We know the dreadful ills that close thee round.

CREUSA
Ah, whither shall I fly? From instant death
Scarce hath my foot sped hither, from my foes
By stealth escaping.

LEADER OF THE CHORUS
Whither wouldst thou fly,
But to this altar?

CREUSA
What will that avail me?

LEADER OF THE CHORUS
To kill a suppliant there the law forbids.

CREUSA
But by the law I perish.

LEADER OF THE CHORUS
If their hands
Had seized thee.

CREUSA
Dreadful contest, with drawn swords
They hastily advance.

LEADER OF THE CHORUS
Now take thy seat
At the altar: shouldst thou die ev'n there, thy blood
Will call the vengeance of the god on those
That spilt it: but our fortune we must bear.

[She takes refuge at the altar as **ION**, **GUARDS**, and **DELPHIANS** enter.]

ION
Bull-visaged sire Cephisus, what a viper
Hast thou produced? a dragon from her eyes
Glaring pernicious flame. Each daring deed
Is hers: less venomous the Gorgon's blood,
With which she purposed to have poison'd me.

Seize her, that the Parnassian rocks may tease
Those nice-adjusted ringlets of her hair,
As down the craggy precipice she bounds.
Here my good genius saved me, e'er I came
To Athens, there beneath my stepdame's wiles
To fall; amid my friends thy fell intents
Have I unravell'd, what a pest to me,
Thy hate how deadly: had thy toils inclosed me
In thine own house, thou wouldst at once have sent me
With complete ruin to the shades below.
But nor the altar nor Apollo's shrine
Shall save thee. Pity, might her voice be heard,
Would rather plead for me and for my mother,
She absent, yet the name remains with me.
Behold that sorceress; with what art she wove
Wile after wile; the altar of the god
Impress'd her not with awe, as if secure.
No vengeance waited her unhallow'd deeds.

CREUSA
I charge thee, kill me not, in my own right,
And in the god's, whose suppliant here I stand.

ION
What right hast thou to plead Apollo's name?

CREUSA
My person hallow'd to the god I offer.

ION
Yet wouldst thou poison one that is the god's.

CREUSA
Thou wast no more Apollo's, but thy father's.

ION
I have been, of a father's wealth I speak.

CREUSA
And now I am: thou hast that claim no more.

ION
But thou art impious: pious were my deeds.

CREUSA
As hostile to my house, I would have kill'd thee.

ION

Did I against thy country march in arms?

CREUSA
And more; thou wouldst have fired Erechtheus' house.

ION
What torch, what brands, what flames had I prepared?

CREUSA
There wouldst thou fix, seizing my right by force.

ION
The land which he possess'd, my father gave me.

CREUSA
What claim hath there the race of Aeolus?

ION
He was its guardian, not with words but arms.

CREUSA
Its soldier then; an inmate, not its lord.

ION
Wouldst thou, through fear of what might happen, kill me?

CREUSA
Lest death should be my portion, if not thine.

ION
Childless thou enviest that my father found me.

CREUSA
And wilt thou make a childless house thy spoil?

ION
Devolves my father then no share to me?

CREUSA
His shield, his spear; be those thine heritage.

ION
Come from the altar, quit that hallow'd seat.

CREUSA
Instruct thy mother, whosoe'er she be.

ION

Shalt thou unpunish'd meditate my death?

CREUSA
Within this shrine if thou wilt murder me.

ION
What pleasure mid these sacred wreaths to die?

CREUSA
We shall grieve one, by whom we have been grieved.

ION
Strange, that the god should give these laws to men,
Bearing no stamp of honour, nor design'd
With provident thought: it is not meet to place
The unrighteous at his altars; worthier far
To be chased thence; nor decent that the vile
Should with their touch pollute the gods: the good,
Oppress'd with wrongs, should at those hallow'd seats
Seek refuge: ill beseems it that the unjust
And just alike should seek protection there.

[As **ION** and his followers are about to tear **CREUSA** from the altar, the **PRIESTESS** of Apollo enters from the temple.]

PRIESTESS
Forbear, my son, leaving the oracular seat,
I pass this pale, the priestess of the god,
The guardian of the tripod's ancient law,
Call'd to this charge from all the Delphian dames.

ION
Hail, my loved mother, dear, though not my parent.

PRIESTESS
Yet let me have the name, 'tis grateful to me.

ION
Hast thou yet heard their wily trains to kill me?

PRIESTESS
I have; but void of mercy thou dost wrong.

ION
Should I not ruin those that sought my life?

PRIESTESS
Stepdames to former sons are always hostile.

ION
And I to stepdames ill intreated thus.

PRIESTESS
Be not, this shrine now leaving for thy country.

ION
How, then, by thy monition should I act?

PRIESTESS
Go with good omens, pure to Athens go.

ION
All must be pure that kill their enemies.

PRIESTESS
So do not thou: attentive mark my words.

ION
Speak: from good will whate'er thou say'st must flow.

PRIESTESS
Seest thou the vase I hold beneath mine arm?

ION
I see an ancient ark entwined with wreaths.

PRIESTESS
In this long since an infant I received thee.

ION
What say'st thou? New is thy discourse and strange.

PRIESTESS
In silence have I kept them: now I show them.

ION
And why conceal'd, as long since thou received'st me?

PRIESTESS
The god would have thee in his shrine a servant.

ION
Is that no more his will? How shall I know it?

PRIESTESS
Thy father shown, he sends thee from this land.

ION
Hast thou preserved these things by charge, or how?

PRIESTESS
It was the god that so disposed my thought.

ION
With what design? Speak, finish thy discourse.

PRIESTESS
Ev'n to this hour to keep what then I found.

ION
What gain imports this to me, or what loss?

PRIESTESS
There didst thou lie wrapp'd in thy infant vests.

ION
Thou hast produced whence I may find my mother.

PRIESTESS
Since now the god so wills, but not before.

ION
This is a day of bless'd discoveries.

PRIESTESS
Now take them: o'er all Asia, and the bounds
Of Europe hold thy progress: thou shalt know
These tokens. To do pleasure to the god,
I nurtured thee, my son; now to thy hand
Restore what was his will I should receive
Unbidden, and preserve: for what intent
It was his will, I have not power to say.
That I had these, or where they were conceal'd,
No mortal knew. And now farewell: the love
I bear thee equals what a parent feels.
Let thy inquiries where they ought begin;
First, if some Delphian virgin gave thee birth,
And in this shrine exposed thee; next, if one
Of Greece. From me, and from the god, who feels
An interest in thy fortune, thou hast all.

[She goes into the temple after giving **ION** the ark.]

ION

Ah me! the moist tear trickles from mine eye,
When I reflect that she who gave me birth,
By stealth espoused, may with like secrecy
Have sold me, to my infant lips her breast
Denied: but in the temple of the god
Without a name, a servile life I led.
All from the god was gracious, but from fortune
Harsh; for the time when in a mother's arms
I in her fondness should have known some joy
Of life, from that sweet care was I estranged,
A mother's nurture: nor less wretched she,
Thus forced to lose the pleasure in her son.
But I will take this vase, and to the god
Bear it, a hallow'd offering; that from thence
I may find nothing which I would not find.
Should she, that gave me being, chance to be
A slave, to find her were a greater ill,
Than to rest silent in this ignorance.
O Phoebus, in thy temple hang I this.
What am I doing? War I not against
The pleasure of the god, who saved for me
These pledges of my mother? I must dare,
And open these: my fate cannot be shunn'd.

[He opens the ark.]

Ye sacred garlands, what have you so long
Conceal'd: ye bands, that keep these precious relics?
Behold the cover of this circular vase;
Its freshness knows no change, as if a god
So will'd; this osier-woven ark yet keeps
Its soundness undecay'd; yet many a year,
Since it contain'd this treasured charge, has pass'd.

CREUSA
What an unhoped-for sight do I behold!

ION
I thought thou long hadst known to keep thee silent.

CREUSA
Silence is mine no more; instruct not me;
For I behold the ark, wherein of old
I laid thee, O my son, an infant babe;
And in the caves of Cecrops, with the rocks
Of Macrai roof'd, exposed thee: I will quit
This altar, though I run on certain death.

ION
Seize her; for by the impulse of the god
She leaves the sculptured altar: bind her bands.

CREUSA
Instantly kill me, so that I embrace
This vase, and thee, and these thy conceal'd pledges.

ION
Is not this strange? I take thee at thy word.

CREUSA
Not strange: a friend thou by thy friends art found.

ION
Thy friend! Yet wouldst thou kill me secretly.

CREUSA
My son: if that to parents is most dear.

ION
Forbear thy wiles; I shall refute them well.

CREUSA
Might I but to come to what I wish, my son!

ION
Is this vase empty, or contains it aught?

CREUSA
Thy infant vests, in which I once exposed thee.

ION
And wilt thou name them to me, ere thou see them?

CREUSA
If I recount them not, be death my meed.

ION
Speak then: thy confidence hath something strange.

CREUSA
A tissue, look, which when a child I wrought.

ION
What is it? Various are the works of virgins.

CREUSA

A slight, unfinish'd essay of the loom.

ION
What figure wrought? Thou shalt not take me thus.

CREUSA
A Gorgon central in the warp enwoven-

ION
What fortune haunts me, O supreme of gods!

CREUSA
And like an aegis edged with serpents round.

ION
Such is the woof, and such the vest I find.

CREUSA
Thou old embroidery of my virgin bands!

ION
Is there aught else besides this happy proof?

CREUSA
Two dragons, an old work, their jaws of gold.

ION
The gift of Pallas, who thus nurtures children?

CREUSA
Emblems of Erichthonius of old times.

ION
Why? for what use? Explain these works of gold.

CREUSA
For ornaments to grace the infant's neck.

ION
See, here they are; the third I wish to know.

CREUSA
A branch of olive then I wreathed around thee,
Pluck'd from that tree which from Minerva's rock
First sprung; if it be there, it still retains
Its verdure: for the foliage of that olive,
Fresh in immortal beauty, never fades.

ION
O my dear mother! I with joy behold thee.
With transport 'gainst thy cheek my cheek recline.

[They embrace.]

CREUSA
My son, my son, far dearer to thy mother
Than yon bright orb (the god will pardon me),
Do I then hold thee in my arms, thus found
Beyond my hopes, when in the realms below,
I thought thy habitation 'mong the dead?

ION
O my dear mother, in thy arms I seem
As one that had been dead to life return'd.

CREUSA
Ye wide-expanded rays of heavenly light,
What notes, what high-raised strains shall tell my joy?
This pleasure whence, this unexpected transport?

ION
There was no blessing farther from my thoughts
Than this, my mother, to be found thy son.

CREUSA
I tremble yet.

ION
And hast thou yet a fear,
Holding me, not to hold me?

CREUSA
Such fond hopes
Long time have I renounced. Thou hallow'd matron,
From whom didst thou receive my infant child?
What bless'd hand brought him to Apollo's shrine?

ION
It was the god's appointment: may our life
To come be happy, as the past was wretched.

CREUSA
Not without tears, my son, wast thou brought forth;
Nor without anguish did my hands resign thee.
Now breathing on thy cheek I feel a joy
Transporting me with heartfelt ecstasies.

ION
The words expressive of thy joys speak mine.

CREUSA
Childless no more, no more alone, my house
Now shines with festive joy; my realms now own
A lord; Erechtheus blooms again; no more
His high-traced lineage sees night darkening round,
But glories in the sun's refulgent beams.

ION
Now let my father, since he's present here,
Be partner of the joy which I have given you.

CREUSA
What says my son?

ION
Such, such as I am proved.

CREUSA
What mean thy words? Far other is thy birth.

ION
Ah me! thy virgin bed produced me base.

CREUSA
Nor bridal torch, my son, nor bridal dance
Had graced my nuptial rites, when thou wast born.

ION
Then I'm a wretch, a base-born wretch: say whence.

CREUSA
Be witness, thou by whom the Gorgon died,-

ION
What means this adjuration?

CREUSA
Who hast fix'd
High o'er my cave thy seat amid the rocks
With olive clothed.

ION
Abstruse thy words, and dark.

CREUSA
Where on the cliffs the nightingale attunes
Her songs, Apollo-

ION
Why Apollo named?

CREUSA
Led me in secret to his bed.

ION
Speak on;
Thy words import some glorious fortune to me.

CREUSA
Thee in the tenth revolving month, my son,
A secret pang to Phoebus did I bear.

ION
Thy words, if true, are grateful to my soul.

CREUSA
These swathing bands, thy mother's virgin work,
Wove by my flying shuttle, round thy body
I roll'd; but from thy lips my breast withheld,
A mother's nouriture, nor bathed thy bands
In cleansing lavers; but to death exposed thee,
Laid in the dreary cave, to birds of prey
A feast, rent piecemeal by their ravenous beaks.

ION
Cruel, my mother, was thy deed.

CREUSA
By fear
Constrain'd, my son, I cast thy life away;
Unwillingly I left thee there to die.

ION
And from my hands unholy were thy death.

CREUSA
Dreadful was then my fortune, dreadful here,
Whirl'd by the eddying blast from misery there
To misery here, and back again to joy:
Her boisterous winds are changed; may she remain
In this repose: enough of ills are past:
After the storm soft breathes a favouring gale.

LEADER OF THE CHORUS
From this example, mid the greatest ills
Never let mortal man abandon hope.

ION
O thou, that hast to thousands wrought a change
Of state ere this, involving them in ills,
And raising them to happiness again;
Fortune, to what a point have I been carried,
Ready to kill my mother, horrid thought!
But in the sun's bright course each day affords
Instruction. Thee, my mother, have I found,
In that discovery bless'd; nor hath my birth
Aught I can blame: yet one thing would I say
To thee alone:-walk this way: to thine ear
In secret would I whisper this, and throw
The veil of darkness o'er each circumstance.
Take heed, my mother, lest thy maiden fault
Seeks in these secret nuptials to conceal
Its fault, then charges on the god the deed;
And, fearing my reproach, to Phoebus gives
A son, to Phoebus whom thou didst not bear.

CREUSA
By her, who 'gainst the giants in her car
Fought by the side of Jove, victorious Pallas,
No one of mortal race is father to thee,
But he who brought thee up, the royal Phoebus.

ION
Why give his son then to another father?
Why say that I was born the son of Xuthus?

CREUSA
Not born the son of Xuthus; but he gives thee,
Born from himself as friend to friend may give
His son, and heir adopted to his house.

ION
True is the god, his tripod else were vain.
Not without cause then is my mind perplex'd.

CREUSA
Hear what my thoughts suggest: to work thee good
Apollo placed thee in a noble house.
Acknowledged his, the rich inheritance
Could not be thine, nor could a father's name;

For I conceal'd my nuptials, and had plann'd
To kill thee secretly: for this the god
In kindness gives thee to another father.

ION
My mind is prompt to entertain such thoughts;
But, entering at his shrine will I inquire
If from a mortal father I am sprung,
Or from Apollo.-Ha! what may this be?
What god above the hallow'd dome unveils
His radiant face that shines another sun?
Haste, let us fly: the presence of the gods
'Tis not for mortals to behold, and live.

[**MINERVA** appears from above.)

MINERVA
Fly not; in me no enemy you fly;
At Athens friendly to you, and no less
Here. From that land I come, so named from me,
By Phoebus sent with speed: unmeet he deems it
To show himself before you, lest with blame
The past be mention'd; this he gave in charge,
To tell thee that she bore thee, and to him,
Phoebus thy father; he to whom he gave thee,
Not as to the author of thy being gives thee,
But to the inheritance of a noble house.
This declaration made, lest thou shouldst die,
Kill'd by thy mother's wily trains, or she
By thee, these means to save you he devised.
These things in silence long conceal'd, at Athens
The royal Phoebus would have made it known
That thou art sprung from her, thy father he:
But to discharge my office, and unfold
The oracle of the god, for which you yoked
Your chariots, hear: Creusa, take thy son,
Go to the land of Cecrops: let him mount
The royal throne; for, from Erechtheus sprung,
That honour is his due, the sovereignty
Over my country: through the states of Greece
Wide his renown shall spread; for from his root
Four sons shall spring, that to the land, the tribes,
The dwellers on my rock, shall give their names.
Geleon the first, Hopletes, Argades,
And from my aegis named Aegicores:
Their sons in fate's appointed time shall fix
Their seats along the coast, or in the isles
Girt by the Aegean sea, and to my land

Give strength; extending thence the opposite plains
Of either continent shall make their own,
Europe and Asia, and shall boast their name
Ionians, from the honour'd Ion call'd.
To thee by Xuthus shall a son be born,
Dorus, from whom the Dorian state shall rise
To high renown; in the Pelopian land,
Another near the Rhian cliffs, along
The sea-wash'd coast, his potent monarchy
Shall stretch, Achaeus; and his subject realms
Shall glory in their chief's illustrious name.
Well hath Apollo quitted him in all:
First, without pain he caused thee bear a son.
That from thy friends thou mightst conceal his birth;
After the birth, soon as his infant limbs
Thy hands had clothed, to Mercury he gave
The charge to take the babe, and in his arms
Convey him hither; here with tenderness
He nurtured him, nor suffer'd him to perish.
Guard now the secret that he is thy son,
That his opinion Xuthus may enjoy
Delighted: thou too hast thy blessings, lady.
And now, farewell: from this relief from ills
A prosperous fortune I to both announce.

ION
O Pallas, daughter of all-powerful Jove!
Not with distrust shall we receive thy words:
I am convinced that Phoebus is my father,
My mother she, not unassured before.

CREUSA
Hear me too, now: Phoebus I praise, before
Unpraised; my son he now restores, of whom
Till now I deem'd him heedless. Now these gates
Are beauteous to mine eyes; his oracles
Now grateful to my soul, unpleasant late.
With rapture on these sounding rings my hands
Now hang; with rapture I address the gates.

MINERVA
This I approve, thy former wayward thoughts
Resign'd, with honour that thou name the god.
Slow are the gifts of Heaven, but found at length
Not void of power.

CREUSA
My son, let us now go

To Athens.

MINERVA
Go; myself will follow you.

CREUSA
A noble guard, and friendly to the state.

MINERVA
But seat him high on thy paternal throne.

CREUSA
A rich possession, and I glory in him.

[**MINERVA** disappears.)

CHORUS [singing)
Son of Latona and all-powerful Jove,
Apollo, hail! Though fortune's blackest storms
Rage on his house, the man whose pious soul
Reveres the gods, assumes a confidence,
And justly: for the good at length obtain
The meed of virtue; but the unholy wretch
(Such is his nature) never can be happy.

Euripides – A Short Biography

Euripides is rightly lauded as one of the great dramatists of all time. In his lifetime, he wrote over 90 plays and although only 18 have survived they reveal the scope and reach of his genius.

Euripides is identified with many theatrical innovations that have influenced drama all the way down to modern times, especially in the representation of traditional, mythical heroes as ordinary people in extraordinary circumstances. This new approach led him to pioneer developments that later writers would adapt to comedy. Yet he also became "the most tragic of poets", focusing on the inner lives and motives of his characters in a way previously unknown. He was "the creator of...that cage which is the theatre of Shakespeare's Othello, Racine's Phèdre, of Ibsen and Strindberg," in which "...imprisoned men and women destroy each other by the intensity of their loves and hates", and yet he was also the literary ancestor of comic dramatists as diverse as Menander and George Bernard Shaw.

As would be expected from a life lived 2,500 years ago, details of it are few and far between. Accounts of his life, written down the ages, do exist but whether much is reliable or surmised is open to debate.

Most accounts agree that he was born on Salamis Island around 480 BC, to mother Cleito and father Mnesarchus, a retailer who lived in a village near Athens. Upon the receipt of an oracle saying that his son was fated to win "crowns of victory", Mnesarchus insisted that the boy should train for a career in athletics.

His education was not only confined to athletics: he also studied painting and philosophy under the masters Prodicus and Anaxagoras.

However, what became quickly very clear was that athletics was not to be his way to win crowns of victory. Euripides had been lucky enough to have been born in the era as the other two masters of Greek Tragedy; Sophocles and Æschylus. It was in their footsteps that he was destined to follow.

His first play was performed some thirteen years after the first of Socrates plays and a mere three years after Æschylus had written his classic The Oristria.

Theatre was becoming a very important part of the Greek culture. The Dionysia, held annually, was the most important festival of theatre and second only to the fore-runner of the Olympic games, the Panathenia, held every four years, in its appeal. It was a large festival in ancient Athens in honor of the god Dionysus, the central events of which were the theatrical performances of dramatic tragedies and, from 487 BC, comedies. The Dionysia actually consisted of two related festivals, the Rural Dionysia and the City Dionysia, which took place in different parts of the year.

Euripides first competed in the City Dionysia, in 455 BC, one year after the death of Æschylus, and, incredibly, it was not until 441 BC that he won first prize. His final competition in Athens was in 408 BC. However, The Bacchae and Iphigenia in Aulis were performed after his death in 405 BC and first prize was awarded posthumously. Altogether his plays won first prize only five times.

His plays, and those of Æschylus and Sophocles, indicate a difference in outlook between the three men, most easily explained as a generational gap, although with three great talents overlapping the driving forces may have pushed individual styles onwards perhaps faster than they may otherwise have done. Æschylus still looked back to the archaic period, Sophocles was in transition between periods, and Euripides was fully bonded with the new spirit of the classical age. When Euripides' plays are sequenced in time, they also show a developing pattern:

An early period of high tragedy (Medea, Hippolytus)
A patriotic period at the outset of the Peloponnesian War (Children of Hercules, Suppliants)
A middle period of disillusionment at the senselessness of war (Hecuba, Women of Troy)
An escapist period with a focus on romantic intrigue (Ion, Iphigenia in Tauris, Helen)
A final period of tragic despair (Orestes, Phoenician Women, Bacchae)

However, with over three quarters of his plays lost it is difficult to be certain as to whether the other works would also represent this development (e.g., Iphigenia at Aulis is dated with the 'despairing' Bacchae, yet it contains elements that became typical of New Comedy). In the Bacchae, he restores the chorus and messenger speech to their traditional role in the tragic plot, and the play appears to be the culmination of a regressive or archaizing tendency in his later works.

In one of his earliest surviving plays, Medea, includes a speech that he seems to have written in defence of himself as an intellectual ahead of his time, and to further challenge the times he has put the words in the mouth of the play's heroine:

"If you introduce new, intelligent ideas to fools, you will be thought frivolous, not intelligent. On the other hand, if you do get a reputation for surpassing those who are supposed to be intellectually sophisticated, you will seem to be a thorn in the city's flesh. This is what has happened to me."—Medea.

As we know Athenian tragedies during Euripides' lifetime were a public contest between playwrights. The state funded that contest and awarded prizes to the winners. The language was spoken and sung verse, the performance area included a circular floor or orchestra where the chorus could dance, a space for actors (usually three speaking actors in Euripides' time), a backdrop or skene and some special effects: an ekkyklema (used to bring the skene's "indoors" outdoors) and a mechane (used to lift actors in the air, as in deus ex machina). With the introduction of the third actor (an innovation attributed to Sophocles), acting also began to be regarded as a skill to be rewarded with prizes, requiring a long apprenticeship in the chorus. Euripides and other playwrights accordingly composed more and more arias for accomplished actors to sing and this tendency becomes more marked in his later plays: tragedy for him was a living and ever-changing genre.

Accounts by the famed comic poet, Aristophanes, characterise Euripides as a spokesman for destructive, new ideas, that mirror or help to bring about declining standards in both society and tragedy. However, 5th century tragedy was a social gathering for "carrying out quite publicly the maintenance and development of mental infrastructure" and it offered spectators a "platform for an utterly unique form of institutionalized discussion". A dramatist's role was not just to entertain but also to educate his fellow citizens—he was expected to have a message. Clearly this use of drama to democratize discussion was a very useful tool for all sides. Traditional myth provided the subject matter but the dramatist was meant to be innovative so as to sustain interest, which led to novel characterization of heroic figures and to use the mythical past to talk about present issues. The difference between Euripides and his older colleagues was, again, one of degree: his characters talked about the present more controversially and more pointedly than did those of Æschylus and Sophocles, sometimes even challenging the democratic order. Thus, for example, Odysseus is represented in Hecuba as "agile-minded, sweet-talking, demos-pleasing" i.e., a type of the war-time demagogues that were active in Athens during the Peloponnesian War. His concept is pleasingly simple. He retains the old stories and myths as well as the great names of the past and places them in the lives of contemporary Athenians thereby immediately help the audience understand it from the point of view of their own lives.

As mouthpieces for contemporary issues, they all seem to have had at least an elementary course in public speaking. Sometimes the dialogue often contrasts so strongly with the mythical and heroic setting, it looks as if Euripides aimed at parody, as for example in The Trojan Women, where the heroine's rationalized prayer provokes comment from Menelaus:

Hecuba:...O Zeus, whether you are the Law of Necessity in nature, or the Law of Reason in man, hear my prayers. You are everywhere, pursuing your noiseless path, ordering the affairs of mortals according to justice.

Menelaus: What's this? You are starting a new fashion in prayer.

Athenian citizens were familiar with rhetoric in the assembly and law courts, and some scholars believe that Euripides was more interested in his characters as speakers with cases to argue than as characters with lifelike personalities. They are self-conscious about speaking formally and their rhetoric is shown to be flawed, as if Euripides was exploring the problematical nature of language and communication: "For speech points in three different directions at once, to the speaker, to the person addressed, to the features in the world it describes, and each of these directions can be felt as skewed". Thus in the example above, Hecuba presents herself as a sophisticated intellectual describing a rationalised cosmos yet the speech is ill-matched to her audience, Menelaus (an unsophisticated listener), and soon it is found not to suit the cosmos either (her infant grandson is brutally murdered by the victorious Greeks).

Æschylus and Sophocles were innovative, but Euripides could move easily between tragic, comic, romantic and political effects, a versatility that appears in individual plays and also over the course of his career. Potential for comedy lay in his use of 'contemporary' characters, in his sophisticated tone, his relatively informal Greek, and his ingenious use of plots centered on motifs that later became standard, such as the 'recognition scene'. Other tragedians also used recognition scenes but they were heroic in emphasis, as in Æschylus's The Libation Bearers, which Euripides parodied with his mundane treatment of it in Electra (Euripides was unique among the tragedians in incorporating theatrical criticism in his plays). Traditional myth, with its exotic settings, heroic adventures and epic battles, offered potential for romantic melodrama as well as for political comments on a war theme, so that his plays are an extraordinary mix of elements. The Trojan Women for example is a powerfully disturbing play on the theme of war's horrors, apparently critical of Athenian imperialism (it was composed in the aftermath of the Melian massacre and during the preparations for the Sicilian Expedition) yet it features the comic exchange between Menelaus and Hecuba quoted above and the chorus considers Athens, the "blessed land of Theus", to be a desirable refuge—such complexity and ambiguity are typical both of his "patriotic" and "anti-war" plays.

Tragic poets in the 5th century competed against one another at the City Dionysia, each with a tetralogy consisting of three tragedies and a satyr-play. The few extant fragments of satyr-plays attributed to Æschylus and Sophocles indicate that these were a loosely structured, simple and jovial form of entertainment. However, in Cyclops (the only complete Euripides satyr-play that survives) the entertainment is structured more like a tragedy and introduced a note of critical irony typical of his other work. His genre-bending inventiveness is shown above all in Alcestis, a blend of tragic and satyric elements. This fourth play in his tetralogy for 438 BC (i.e., it occupied the position conventionally reserved for satyr-plays) is a "tragedy" that features Heracles as a satyric hero in conventional satyr-play scenes, involving an arrival, a banquet, a victory over an ogre (in this case, Death), a happy ending, a feast and a departure to new adventures.

Euripides was also a great lyric poet. In Medea, for example, he composed for his city, Athens, "the noblest of her songs of praise". His lyric skills however are not just confined to individual poems: "A play of Euripides is a musical whole....one song echoes motifs from the preceding song, while introducing new ones."

Much of his life and his whole career coincided with the struggle between Athens and Sparta for hegemony in Greece but he didn't live to see the final defeat of his city.

It is said that he died in Macedonia after being attacked by the Molossian hounds of King Archelaus and that his cenotaph near Piraeus was struck by lightning—signs of his unique powers, whether for good or ill. In an account by Plutarch, the complete failure of the Sicilian expedition led Athenians to trade renditions of Euripides' lyrics to their enemies in return for food and drink (Life of Nicias 29). Plutarch is the source also for the story that the victorious Spartan generals, having planned the demolition of Athens and the enslavement of its people, grew merciful after being entertained at a banquet by lyrics from Euripides' play Electra: "they felt that it would be a barbarous act to annihilate a city which produced such men" (Life of Lysander).

In The Frogs, composed after Euripides and Æschylus were both dead, Aristophanes imagines the god Dionysus venturing down to Hades in search of a good poet to bring back to Athens. After a debate between the two deceased bards, the god brings Æschylus back to life as more useful to Athens on account of his wisdom, rejecting Euripides as merely clever. Such comic 'evidence' suggests that Athenians admired Euripides even while they mistrusted his intellectualism, at least during the long war with Sparta.

Euripides had a famous library—one of the first to be privately collected. Although he lived most of his life in the midst of the cultured society of Athens, and was in some respects a leader in it, he grew bitter and despondent over the fierce rivalries and greedy ambitions which ran through the city. He loved the seclusion of his house at Salamis, where it was said that he composed his dramas in a cave.

Euripides fell out of favour with his fellow Athenian citizens and retired to the court of Archelaus, king of Macedon, who treated him with consideration and affection.

At his death, in around 406BC, he was mourned by the king, who, refusing the request of the Athenians that his remains be carried back to the Greek city, buried him with much splendor within his own dominions. His tomb was placed at the confluence of two streams, near Arethusa in Macedonia, and a cenotaph was built to his memory on the road from Athens towards the Piraeus.

Euripides – A Concise Bibliography

Alcestis (438 BC)
Medea (431 BC)
Heracleidae (c. 430 BC)
Hippolytus (428 BC)
Andromache (c. 425 BC)
Hecuba (c. 424 BC)
The Suppliants (c. 423 BC)
Electra (c. 420 BC)
Heracles (c. 416 BC)
The Trojan Women (c. 415 BC)
Iphigenia in Tauris (c. 414 BC)
Ion (c. 414 BC)
Helen (c. 412 BC)
Phoenician Women (c. 410 BC)
Orestes (c.408 BC)
Bacchae (405 BC)
Iphigenia at Aulis (405 BC)
Rhesus
Cyclops

Lost and Fragmentary Plays (Dated)

Peliades (455 BC)

Telephus (438 BC with Alcestis)
Alcmaeon in Psophis (438 BC with Alcestis)
Cretan Women (438 with Alcestis)
Cretans (c. 435 BC)
Philoctetes (431 BC with Medea)
Dictys (431 BC with Medea)
Theristai (satyr play, 431 BC with Medea)
Stheneboea (before 429 BC)
Bellerophon (c. 430 BC)
Cresphontes (ca. 425 BC)
Erechtheus (422 BC)
Phaethon (c. 420 BC)
Wise Melanippe (c. 420 BC)
Alexandros (415 BC with Trojan Women)
Palamedes (415 BC with Trojan Women)
Sisyphus (satyr play, 415 BC with Trojan Women)
Captive Melanippe (c. 412 BC)
Andromeda (412 BC with Helen)
Antiope (c. 410 BC)
Archelaus (c. 410 BC)
Hypsipyle (c. 410 BC)
Alcmaeon in Corinth (c. 405 BC) Won first prize as part of a trilogy with The Bacchae and Iphigenia in Aulis.

Lost and Fragmentary Plays (Not Dated)

Aegeus
Aeolus
Alcmene
Alope, or Cercyon
Antigone
Auge
Autolycus
Busiris
Cadmus
Chrysippus
Danae
Epeius
Eurystheus
Hippolytus Veiled
Ino
Ixion
Lamia
Licymnius
Meleager
Mysians
Oedipus

Oeneus
Oenomaus
Peirithous
Peleus
Phoenix
Phrixus
Pleisthenes
Polyidus
Protesilaus
Reapers
Rhadamanthys
Sciron
Scyrians
Syleus
Temenidae
Temenos
Tennes
Theseus
Thyestes

Printed in Great Britain
by Amazon

63322973R00041